GREATER THAN A TOURIST BOOK SERIES
REVIEWS FROM READERS

I think the series is wonderful and beneficial for tourists to get information before visiting the city.

-Seckin Zumbul, Izmir Turkey

I am a world traveler who has read many trip guides but this one really made a difference for me. I would call it a heartfelt creation of a local guide expert instead of just a guide.

-Susy, Isla Holbox, Mexico

New to the area like me, this is a must have!

-Joe, Bloomington, USA

This is a good series that gets down to it when looking for things to do at your destination without having to read a novel for just a few ideas.

i

-Rachel, Monterey, USA

Good information to have to plan my trip to this destination.

-Pennie Farrell, Mexico

Great ideas for a port day.

-Mary Martin USA

Aptly titled, you won't just be a tourist after reading this book. You'll be greater than a tourist!

-Alan Warner, Grand Rapids, USA

Even though I only have three days to spend in San Miguel in an upcoming visit, I will use the author's suggestions to guide some of my time there. An easy read - with chapters named to guide me in directions I want to go.

-Robert Catapano, USA

Great insights from a local perspective! Useful information and a very good value!

-Sarah, USA

This series provides an in-depth experience through the eyes of a local. Reading these series will help you to travel the city in with confidence and it'll make your journey a unique one.

-Andrew Teoh, Ipoh, Malaysia

GREATER THAN A TOURIST – RHODE ISLAND USA

50 Travel Tips from a Local

Kwana Renee Adams

Cover designed by:

Greater Than a Tourist
Visit our website at www.GreaterThanaTourist.com

Lock Haven, PA
All rights reserved.
ISBN: 9781983271182

>TOURIST

50 TRAVEL TIPS FROM A LOCAL

BOOK DESCRIPTION

Are you excited about planning your next trip?

Do you want to try something new?

Would you like some guidance from a local?

If you answered yes to any of these questions, then this Greater Than a Tourist book is for you.

Greater Than a Tourist- Greater Than a Tourist- Rhode Island USA by Kwana Renee Adams offers the inside scoop on Rhode Island. Most travel books tell you how to travel like a tourist. Although there is nothing wrong with that, as part of the Greater Than a Tourist series, this book will give you travel tips from someone who has lived at your next travel destination.

In these pages, you will discover advice that will help you throughout your stay. This book will not tell you exact addresses or store hours but instead will give you excitement and knowledge from a local that you may not find in other smaller print travel books.

Travel like a local. Slow down, stay in one place, and get to know the people and the culture. By the time you finish this book, you will be eager and prepared to travel to your next destination.

TABLE OF CONTENTS

22. Shop, Eat, Or Watch A Movie At The Providence Place Mall

23. Providence Has A Skating Rink

24. We Can Put Fire On Water

25. Rhode Island Festivals

26. Diversity In The City

27. Stay in Providence if you like the Nightlife

28. Best Hotel Locations Based On Interest

29. Narragansett Is For Tourists Who Love The Beach

30. These Movies Were Shot Here

31. Notable People From Rhode Island

32. Viola Davis

33. For the Sports Fan

34. Historical Landmarks to visit

35. Visit Some Colleges While You're Here

36. Rhode Island School Of Design

37. RISD Museum

38. Notable Alumni of RISD

39. Rhode Island Theater Companies

40. AS220

41. New Urban Arts

42. We've Got Farmers Markets Too

43. Local Bookstores Need Love Too

44. Hope Artiste Village

45. Rhode Island Runs on Dunkin

DEDICATION

This book is dedicated to Rhode Islanders. We always say we want to leave but we always come back if we do.

ABOUT THE AUTHOR

Kwana Renee Adams is a writer born and raised in Providence, Rhode Island. She is a creative soul who loves to create and make things. She loves to read, write, and go running when the weather is nice. She aspires to one day become a cat lady and is already on her way with her cats Bella and Fluffster Cuddles.

HOW TO USE THIS BOOK

The Greater Than a Tourist book series was written by someone who has lived in an area for over three months. The goal of this book is to help travelers either dream or experience different locations by providing opinions from a local. The author has made suggestions based on their own experiences. Please do your own research before traveling to the area in case the suggested places are unavailable.

FROM THE PUBLISHER

Traveling can be one of the most important parts of a person's life. The anticipation and memories that you have are some of the best. As a publisher of the Greater Than a Tourist book series, as well as the popular 50 Things to Know book series, we strive to help you learn about new places, spark your imagination, and inspire you. Wherever you are and whatever you do I wish you safe, fun, and inspiring travel.

Lisa Rusczyk Ed. D.
CZYK Publishing

OUR STORY

Traveling is a passion of the "Greater than a Tourist" series creator. Lisa studied abroad in college, and for their honeymoon Lisa and her husband toured Europe. During her travels to Malta, an older man tried to give her some advice based on his own experience living on the island since he was a young boy. She was not sure if she should talk to the stranger but was interested in his advice. When traveling to some places she was wary to talk to locals because she was afraid that they weren't being genuine. Through her travels, Lisa learned how much locals had to share with tourists. Lisa created the "Greater Than a Tourist" book series to help connect people with locals. A topic that locals are very passionate about sharing.

WELCOME TO
> TOURIST

INTRODUCTION

"Travel makes one modest. You see what a tiny place you occupy in the world"

Gustav Flaubert

Being the smallest state, Rhode Island can sometimes tend to get overlooked. People ask all the time if it's part of New York or if Quahog is really a town. (No and no). Rhode Island is so unique in its own ways. It's rich in art, culture and history. Every city has its own opportunity to learn something new. We may be the smallest state but we've got the biggest personality.

Rhode Island was founded on religious freedom and the state is home to many different religions, cultures, and communities. You can get from one side of the state to the other in an hour or less, but don't that fool you into thinking this state is boring or uneventful. You could spend hours exploring and still be in one city. I've lived in Providence all of my life and I still have not learned all of its secrets. Rhode Island has so much to offer and I'm glad you have picked up the book to learn all about what it is that makes our state so special. Stay tuned as I take you on a tour of Rhode Island's best tourist spots and all they have to offer!

1. BRISTOL IS FOR THE PATRIOTIC

Did you know Bristol was home to the oldest Independence Day Parade? The parade was founded in 1785 and still goes on today! You'll know what street the parade goes down because the streets are painted red, white, and blue, and flags can be seen hanging from almost every home and store front.

Bristol also offers Colt State Park, a beautiful state park where families come to have barbecues, swim and sometimes even have parties! The scenery is beautiful and it's definitely a place to stop and visit when you come to Rhode Island. The park also features a skate park, and trails for joggers and bikers. It's a beautiful place to take the family for a day trip.

Bristol is also home to Roger Williams University which is located on a waterfront. Roger Williams University was, of course, named after the founder of Rhode Island, Roger Williams. Some notable alumni of RWU include, Lovie Austin, Adam Braver, and Jason Mattera.

2. EXETER IS FOR THE PARANORMAL FANS, FOLKLORISTS, AND GHOSTBUSTERS

If you're not freaked out by ghost and vampire stories, you should definitely stop by Exeter. This is the home of the famous Mercy Brown vampire story. In the 19th century, tuberculosis was a frightful disease and some believed that someone in the Brown family was a vampire that was spreading the disease around.

This disease was very misunderstood at the time so a lot of superstitions and spooky stories were spread around. People persuaded a living member of the family to exhume several bodies of the members who died of the disease. Two of the bodies showed signs of decomposition as they should, but one body, the body of Mercy Brown, showed no signs of decomposition.

The people of Exeter believed this was because she was part of the undead so they had her heart burned with the ashes being mixed with water for a family member to drink. The remains of her body are buried in the cemetery of The Baptist Church in Exeter. The real reason for her body not being as decomposed was because she was stored in almost freezer-like conditions in an above ground vault. Some people claim they feel a chill when standing next to her gravestone and some have maybe seen her ghost!

3. RHODE ISLAND IS FOR THRILL SEEKERS

Mercy Brown isn't the only scary story to come out of Rhode Island. This place has many reportedly haunted areas. From ghost sightings, to abandoned schools and hospitals, to vampires, some of these places aren't for the faint of heart. Do you believe in ghosts? Are you afraid of the dark?

The Ladd School is also another paranormal place in Exeter, RI. It was a school to serve the needs of the mentally disabled and developmentally delayed. It was hit with a lot of scandals about health and human rights violations, some that resulted in deaths. Most of the school is demolished but people still visit it to see if it's really haunted. No one is really allowed to visit the ground anymore but a thrill seeker gets in every now and again to witness any paranormal activity.

The inspiration for the movie The Conjuring came from Harrisville, RI. The Real Perron family lived there in a small farmhouse in 1970. The house was haunted by a suspected witch called Bathsheba who was accused of sacrificing an infant to the devil using a knitting needle. It was suspected that she was haunting the house and possessing the inhabitants over the years. The Perron Family called Ed and Lorraine Wilson, paranormal experts, to try and get rid of the spirit. The house is still standing today.

4. THE PROVIDENCE BILTMORE IS HAUNTED

The Biltmore is a great place to stay with beautiful rooms, a great view of the Downtown area and… ghosts? The Biltmore is said to have had many murders occur there and apparently the victims never left. They apparently still haunt the hotel, having parties and slamming doors.

If you look up providence biltmore on Youtube, you'll find some videos of alleged ghosts slamming the doors. The Biltmore itself was allegedly built by a Satanist named Johan Leisse Weisskopf. He had built a chicken coop on the roof for sacrifices among other things before the authorities tore it down. It apparently didn't work in getting rid of the spirits.

All of this can just be speculation and rumor, but I think it's worth it to find out. Despite the unwelcome guests, the Biltmore is a beautiful hotel in a prime downtown location. The rooms are spacious and amazing, the interior of the lobby is amazing as well where the famous glass elevator is on display. It's not in use anymore these days but it's still nice to look at.

5. RHODE ISLAND IS FOR LOVECRAFT FANS

H.P Lovecraft was a horror fiction author born in Providence, RI. Some of his greatest works include, The Rats in The Walls, The Call of Cthulu, and At The Mountains of Madness. He died poor, not gaining much success while he was alive. However, his writing gained a lot more recognition later on.

Lovecraft is buried in Swan Point Cemetery on the East Side of Providence and fans actually raised money to buy a headstone with his name and "I AM PROVIDENCE' engraved on it. He had a large fan base and still does to this day. The area surrounding Swan Point is actually beautiful and picturesque; a wonderful place to be buried.

Lovecraft also happened to be a fan of Edgar Allan Poe who also had some ties to Providence, though he was not born here. They wrote similarly in the genre of horror fiction and gothic styles. Lovecraft found Edgar Allan Poe to be an idol of him. Speaking of Edgar Allan Poe...

6. EDGAR ALLAN POE APPARENTLY HAUNTS THE EAST SIDE OF PROVIDENCE

Poe visited Providence often to visit Sarah Helen Whitman, a woman he was in love with. Sarah Whitman was from Providence and was a writer and a poet among other things. The athenaeum was a popular Providence hang out for the both of them and they spent time there often.

They got engaged after a while but it was troubled and didn't last long. Whitman broke it off with Poe who was unable to stay sober. The athenaeum was the last place they were together. Mr Poe apparently decided he loved Providence so much, he would stay forever.

Although Poe did not die in Providence, people have reported seeing his spiritual figure outside of the athenaeum, where he and Sarah were last together. Some have even reported seeing his ghost inside of the athenaeum where he and Sarah's portraits hang.

This can all be speculation but I think it's well worth a trip to Benefit Street and besides, the athenaeum is a wonderful, magical place to stop while in Providence.

7. VISIT THE PROVIDENCE ATHENAEUM

The Providence Athenaeum is a library filled with books from thc past and present. Originally living in the Providence arcade, it moved to its home on Benefit St where it lives now. It is a wonderful place filled with amazing history.

As I mentioned above, Lovecraft and Poe frequented the athenaeum often. Poe apparently has never left. The library features a bronze bust of Lovecraft on the main floor in memory of the writer. Great minds have been visitors of this place and it's worth the history to visit.

The main library, children's library, and downstairs reading room are open to the public to explore. The library also has a rare book room which can only be accessed by private appointment or booking a tour. Speaking of rare books: the athenaeum has a book with a cover made of human skin! If you're still not convinced about visiting, then I don't know what else I can say!

8. VISIT THE FIRST INDOOR MALL

The Providence Arcade located in the downtown area of Providence was a historic shopping place known as the first indoor shopping mall. It was officially declared a National Historical Landmark in 1976. It closed down, reopened, and now has micro lofts and shopping areas.

The outside of it is a beautiful, large structure that fits well with its surroundings. The inside features 48 micro lofts on the second and third floors and is only accessible by residents of the building. The first floor is accessible to everyone and features shops and restaurants for people to visit.

The retail shops include an eyebrow threading shop, a vintage shop, restaurants and more. Most retail businesses are local to Rhode Island. Stop by Rogue Island Local Kitchen and Bar for some food while you take a break from shopping.

9. EAT LOCALLY

Rhode Island is full of local restaurants that serve the most delicious food. From pizza to burgers to Mediterranean food, there are a lot of options to choose from. Rhode Island is the perfect state for all you foodies!

For our vegetarian visitors, try garden grille, veggie fun, and the Grange. The Grange is located on Broadway, Providence West Side. Veggie Fun is located in Providence's bustling downtown area. Garden Grille is located in Pawtucket, a short distance from Providence.

If you like to watch sports while you eat, stop at the Brass Monkey for burgers, wings, and more delicious menu options. Stop by on a Thursday for 50 cent wings until 12:45 am. I recommend you get there early because they can get slammed and no one wants to wait a half hour to be seated.

If you love Italian food, take a drive down Atwells Ave, also known as Federal Hill or Little Italy and take your pick from dozens of italian restaurants. Stop at Sicilia's for deep dish pizza and wings. Or Venda Ravioli if you're having a craving for pasta. Stop at Trattoria Zooma for gnocchi to die for.

10. NEW YORK SYSTEMS, AWFUL AWFULS, AND COFFEE MILK

While we're on the topic of food, I should mention a few Rhode Island staples that are also to die for. Yes, it's called a New York System but Rhode Islanders have claimed it and love it. It's basically a thin hot dog with meat sauce, onions, mushrooms, and celery salt. I know some of you are thinking that probably sounds disgusting, but it's actually delicious. Don't knock it 'til you try it!

Awful Awfuls are actually anything but awful. An Awful Awful is basically a milkshake but it's also not. The ingredients are whole milk, flavored syrup and frozen ice milk to create a sweet concoction. If you're looking for where to get one, there are plenty of Newport Creamery restaurants scattered across the state, so don't forget to grab yourself one!

If you're not really a milkshake person, you can try come coffee milk. No, it isn't coffee with milk in it. It's coffee syrup, similar to the chocolate syrup used to make chocolate milk. It's a delicious and refreshing drink that you can make at home. Most grocery stores sell the Autocrat coffee milk syrup for your convenience.

11. PROVIDENCE HAS AN ARCADE BAR

After you enjoy your New York System weiner, stop around the corner and play some games at the Shelter Arcade Bar. As Providence's first and only arcade bar, it IS actually a bar and an arcade. The bar serves drinks and food but the food is only available during certain times of the day. The arcade games are all free except for Skee Ball which is only 25 cents.

The games are for all ages but the bar, obviously, is for 21+ adults. Games include Ms. Pac-Man, Street Fighter 2, and Pinball machine games. There are even two and four player games for some competitive entertainment.

The Shelter Arcade Bar is connected to the Fete Music Hall where various events and concerts occasionally occur. Fete has also been hosting Emo Nights in the Music Hall for all the tortured souls who just wanna rock out and listen to some Emo tunes. The Arcade Bar and Fete Music Hall are a great place to stop for some fun, games, and music.

12. BEST AREAS TO GRAB FOOD IN PROVIDENCE

Thayer St on Providence's East side has a melting pot of delicious restaurants to choose from. Want Chinese food? Try Shanghai for some delicious cuisine. Feeling like having a burrito? Good luck choosing between Chipotle and Baha's! Or want to support a local restaurant? Stop in to Mike's Calzones for some burgers, chicken tenders, and yes, calzones! The food is amazing.

Federal Hill gets another mention because not only does it have a multitude of Italian food, it has even more variety. There's sushi, pizza, pasta, burgers, etc. Not quite in Federal Hill but close to it is Mt Fuji Japanese Steakhouse where you can get the most amazing hibachi. Hibachi is amazing and who doesn't love to watch the chef cook their food?

If you like fine dining, take a drive to Newport and try some delicious food from 41 North, The Landing, or 22 Bowen's. These restaurants have the best that Newport has to offer. Of course, you can grab a burger up there at Brick Alley or some ice cream at Ben and Jerry's on Thames Street. Rhode Island may be small but we're a food state and you'll never go hungry here.

13. NEWPORT IS FOR VACATIONERS

Newport is probably one of the most beautiful areas of Rhode Island. From almost every area, you can get a view of the water and if you don't, Newport is still beautiful wherever you go. So don't worry about where your hotel is going to be, because every hotel in Newport is in an amazing spot.

If you do want a prime ocean view, then book your room at Gurney's Newport Resort and Marina right now. Located on Goat Island, an island off Newport, Gurney's probably has the best view of the ocean in Newport. This hotel also comes with suite rooms and many amenities. It's the perfect spot for a romantic getaway.

If you're looking for a hotel just to dump your stuff on the way to the beaches and restaurants, try the Newport Marriott. It's located close to Goat Island so you still get a view of the water but you're still in a great location. If you're looking for a locally owned bed and breakfast, try the Newport Blues Inn. It's small but cozy and has a homey feeling. It's located within walking distance to Thames Street so it's in a perfect location.

14. NEWPORT IS FOR HISTORY BUFFS

Newport Blues is also located close to Bellevue Ave where most of the historic Newport Mansions live. The names of the Mansions are Rosecliff, Marble House, The Breakers, Chateau Sur Mer, Isaac Bell House, The Elms, Hunter House, Kingscote, Chepstow, and Green Animals which is a topiary garden in Portsmouth. The Mansions are owned and taken care of by the Preservation Society of Newport County and tours are always available.

Some of the mansions are also occasionally rented out for events like weddings and proms. Rosecliff is a very popular, and beautiful place to have a wedding. The backyard provides the perfect space for a reception and wedding photos. The ballroom was built specifically for parties and entertaining guests. It has a great view of the backyard and the ocean. It is the perfect place to have a dream wedding.

Rosecliff originally belonged to Mrs Theresa Fair Oelrichs in 1899. She loved to throw lavish parties there and actually had the mansion built around the large ballroom where she threw her parties. The house is now preserved by the Preservation Society of

Newport County but you can still throw some lavish parties like Ms Tessie Oelrichs.

Marble House once belonged to the very wealthy Vanderbilt family in 1892. It was sold to Frederick H Prince in 1932. It was then gifted to the Preservation Society in 1963 from the Prince estate. Marble House is a beautiful mansion and a National Historical landmark.

15. GO FOR A CLIFFWALK

Marble House, Rosecliff, and The Breakers can be seen from the Cliffwalk in Newport as well as other beautiful homes along the coast. Cliffwalk is a free, public walk along eastern shore of Newport. From one side, you get a view of the vast and beautiful ocean and from the other side, you can see some of the mansions and other large, beautiful homes.

Make sure you wear comfy shoes when you take this adventure. The trail 3.5 miles and occasionally has rock to climb over. I made the mistake of not wearing the right shoes my first time doing the cliff walk and I had to limp my way home. There are a few points where you may stop if you don't wish to continue but I encourage you to walk the whole thing and experience pure, Rhode Island beauty.

There are fences and gates to keep you safe so don't worry about tumbling off the cliff. However, some areas are rockier than others so still take some caution. Belmont to Ledge Road is the most challenging part of Cliffwalk so if you're not up to the challenge, take off before you reach that point. There are maps and trail markers to help you on your way.

16. RHODE ISLAND IS FOR SIGHTSEERS

I don't mean to brag but there are some really beautiful areas of Rhode Island. The aforementioned Cliffwalk and mansions are just the tip of iceberg. There are some truly beautiful areas of Rhode Island that pictures don't do justice. You've gotta come see them for yourself.

The Sakonnet River is another beautiful, scenic area of Rhode Island. Sakonnet River is a saltwater strait that separates Aquidneck Island from the rest of Rhode Island. Aquidneck Island includes Newport, Portsmouth and Middletown. It doesn't matter which side of the river you're on because the whole thing is beautiful.

India Point Park in Providence also deserves honorable mentions as another area of Rhode Island that needs to be explored. It's a public park where you can enjoy a picnic with your family or a festival. Take your bike out and enjoy the scenery as you pedal past. During the Fourth of July holiday, you can also park and enjoy some fireworks.

17. JAMESTOWN, RHODE ISLAND IS FULL OF WONDERS

Do yourself a favor and stop through Jamestown while you explore Rhode Island. It's a beautiful, small town located on Conanicut Island. It is surrounded by water and can only be reached by bridge. After visiting Newport, take the Newport Bridge over to Jamestown to explore.

Fort Wetherill is an amazing spot in Jamestown to visit. I've been there twice myself and have always been amazed. It's a former coast artillery fort filled with tunnels covered in colorful graffiti with beautiful views of nature surrounding it. It now serves as a State Park for families to explore. The park also has public restrooms and picnic tables for when you need a break from all of your exploring.

Once you're done exploring at Fort Wetherill, take a drive over to Beavertail State Park. I can personally vouch for it's beautifulness. You can see the water splashing against the rocks and also have a look at the Beavertail Lighthouse which dates back to 1856! It's a beautiful sightseeing place, especially at sunset. You can get the most breathtaking photos of Beavertail during the sunset. Trust me!

18. BEST RHODE ISLAND BEACHES

Rhode Island isn't called the Ocean State for nothing! Yes, there are places where you can view beautiful oceans but there are spots where you can also swim in them. Rhode Island is known for its beautiful family beaches. Whether you like waves, or a lake beach, we have it all.

Easton's Beach in Newport is a great beach for families. It features a playground, and on site Save the Bay. It's located not too far from the Cliffwalk and mansions so it's in a perfect relationship for a family day trip. Easton's Beach is a great beach and one of the ones to visit in Rhode Island.

Scarborough in Narragansett is my favorite beach and a favorite for anyone who loves waves that can knock you off your feet. They charge a parking fee but it's worth it to spend a day in the waves and the sun. However, if you want a beach that has rocks where you can collect shells, stop by Oakland Beach in Warwick.

East Beach in Watch Hill is a beautiful beach where you can get a nice view of Block Island. It's a great beach for families with teens to hang out on the East Beach Wall and also get knocked over by the waves. It's a public beach but don't get too close to Taylor Swift's summer house unless you want grief from her security team!

19. TAKE A HIKE

If you're not much of a sand and sun person and would rather hit the trails, Rhode Island has some amazing places for hiking. Cliffwalk isn't the only place to go for a great hike. The whole state has great areas where you can hike and enjoy a great view.

Sachuest Point in Middletown is a great hiking trails for beginners. It's relatively flat and less than two miles. It also still has a great view of the ocean so you can go for a great hike without having to brave

33

the Cliffwalk and it's rocky terrains. Don't forget to snap photos of all of the beautiful nature and wildlife.

If you want a good hike, but you're a city slicker like me, take a hike in Neutaconkanut Hill in Providence. Yes, there is still beautiful scenery in our capital city! This area marks the highest spot in Providence and is the perfect place to view beautiful nature and still be in the city.

20. CLAM CAKES, CHOWDER, AND OTHER SEAFOOD

I know some of you have been waiting for this, and yes, we could not be called the Ocean State and not have great seafood. You will probably never find better Clam Cakes and clam chowder outside of Iggy's. New England clam chowder isn't exclusive to Rhode Island but we make it the best, especially at Iggy's. It's creamy, delicious and has plenty of nice sized clam and potato chunks.

Iggy's is located in Warwick on Oakland Beach and also has a storefront in Narragansett. The clam cakes are delicious, and always cooked to perfection. They also have the perfect amount of clam chunks and, if made correctly, are perfectly buttery and crunchy. Don't leave Rhode Island without trying the clam cakes and clam chowder.

Of course there is more seafood to be had than clam cakes and chowder. If you're looking for a good lobster roll, Hemenways, Providence Oyster bar, and Matunuck Oyster Bar have got you covered. It doesn't really matter where you get a lobster roll as long as you get one from a locally owned Rhode Island seafood restaurant. You won't be disappointed but we will if you don't try locally made seafood.

21. SPEND LOCALLY

Speaking of local, make sure to support local businesses while you're visiting. Rhode Island is full of local shops where you can get your standard local tourist t shirts, mugs and keychains. However, there are businesses that don't sell those things but still deserve your business.

If you're looking to get your hair or nails done, there's practically a salon on every street. For a great blowout, drive down Broad Street in Providence and you'll find dozens of salons to make you look great. There are so many, it's too much to name but the prices are usually in the same range and no matter where you go, you can expect to sit there for a while but the wait is worth it. Porto Pelo is a very popular Providence salon where we've all been going to get our hair done since we were children.

The Providence place mall has two nail salons that does an amazing job on nails and toes. The staff at Foxy Nails and Golden Nails are sweet and will take care of you and your nails. Make sure you stop by and support these local nail salons so that they may continue to serve the population.

22. SHOP, EAT, OR WATCH A MOVIE AT THE PROVIDENCE PLACE MALL

The Providence Place Mall has many amazing things for you and the family to do. Feel like having sushi? They've got that! How about chicken or sandwiches? They've got that too! Maybe you want a Johnny Rocket burger. Well you're in luck cause they've got that too.

What else does the mall have? How about a movie theater and an IMAX? We all know movie theater snack prices are through the roof but I say the popcorn is worth it. The IMAX and theater seats are comfy and make for a relaxing movie watching experience.

If you're not up for a movie, stop across the hall to Dave and Buster's to play some games. Dave and Buster's is fun no matter what age you are. They have food, games, and super fun prizes. Even if you don't win thousands of tickets, you can still get some candy from the prize shop.

23. PROVIDENCE HAS A SKATING RINK

If the mall isn't really your scene, you can walk over to downtown and visit the outdoor skating rink. In the summer, when it's dry, it's a popular place for skateboarding. Recently, they've introduced bumper cars which have proven to be so popular, they decided to keep the as a permanent thing!

In the winter, it's an ice skating rink, a fun activity for families and couples. They also offer lessons if you're not familiar with ice skating but still want to learn. Skating on the ice while music plays is a perfect activity while you're visiting Rhode Island.

24. WE CAN PUT FIRE ON WATER

Yes, you read that correctly. In Providence, we celebrate something we call a Waterfire where we actually put fire on top of water. It's something you have to see to believe.

The waterfire is a festival that was introduced by Barnaby Evans and blossomed into a huge family friendly festival. There's local talent, great food, and human statues. The waterfire is a free event for the public but as they are a nonprofit, donations are very much ecnouraged.

So how do we put the fire on water? Well, to explain it as best as I could, the water fire is performed on the Providence River where basins on top of the water are filled with fire. Entertainers go out on gondolas and sometimes throw flowers into the crowd and play with fire themselves. It really is something you have to see for yourself.

25. RHODE ISLAND FESTIVALS

Waterfire isn't the only festival that Rhode Island hosts. There are some truly amazing festivals that go on here. We've got cultural festivals, festivals celebrating history, plus more.

Newport has plenty of festivals itself. The flower festival, at the Rosecliff mansion, is a festival that you can participate. Newport also is home to the Reggae festival every year as well as the Folk festival. Rhode Island also hosts an International Film Festival.

For cultural festivals, Rhode Island offers the Cape Verdean festival every year as well as the Dominican and Puerto Rican festivals. These are great festivals for delicious food, and cultural celebrations. Thousands of people come out every year to celebrate these cultures. You don't have to be part of the culture to celebrate and that's part of the beauty.

26. DIVERSITY IN THE CITY

If you're looking to visit a great, diverse city, look no further than Providence. Providence is one of the best cities for LGBT community (We were ranked 4th most LGBT city in the US!). We host the Pride festival every June and it's an amazing time filled with inclusion, partying and.. pride!

Providence also has numerous LGBT clubs such as EGO, Dark Lady, Alley Cat, Mirabar, and more. You don't have to be LGBT to go to these clubs, they're for everyone! They play an array of good music so there's something to suit everyone's taste. Most of these clubs are in the downtown area so they're conveniently located next to food spots and other clubs.

Even if you're just visiting for a short while, there are still many chances to find an LGBT friendly event. Sometimes there are meetups or brunches or some good old fashioned dance parties. Providence's LGBT community is very welcoming and surely won't mind if you're in town and want to hang out and network with people. Try to see if there are any LGBT events going on while you're staying in town.

27. STAY IN PROVIDENCE IF YOU LIKE THE NIGHTLIFE

While we're on the topic of clubs, Providence has a very bustling nightlife. If that's something you're interested in, consider finding lodging in Providence. There are tons of clubs that play all types of music for all the varying tastes. Most clubs are downtown and conveniently located in the city center.

If you're into hip hop and dance hall style music, try Ultra Nightclub. They play a variety of music but mostly the aforementioned genres. This clubs also has two sections so if you're not feeling a certain DJ, slide over to the other side and listen to what they're playing over there.

If you're into techno/EDM/House music, you may like Colosseum or Dark Lady. These clubs also mix up the genres of music but it is mostly the aforementioned genres that they play. Both Ultra and Colosseum have a cover charge to get into the club.

If you like free clubs and a true mix of genres, try The Salon. The Salon is more of a bar with a dance floor and it has two floors, two DJS and two bartenders. If downstairs DJ isn't playing something you like, try upstairs DJ. Their music selection is a

41

little more diverse and you may occasionally hear some 90s pop tunes mixed in.

28. BEST HOTEL LOCATIONS BASED ON INTEREST

If you'd like to stay in Providence during your visit, there are plenty of hotels to choose from. If you'd like to stay close to public transit, there are a few hotels in the downtown area perfect for you. If you'd like to remain close to downtown but not exactly in it, there's a Marriott just right outside of downtown and close to the train station.

If you'd like to be smack dab in the middle of downtown, the Omni, Hilton, and the Haunted Biltmore are great for you. The Omni hotel connects to the mall and the convention center if you'd like to be close to the action. The Biltmore is connected to a bar and Starbucks if you'd just love to leave your room to grab a quick drink.

If you'd like a hotel near the water, Newport is your destination. Aside from the ones mentioned above, Newport has plenty of more hotels to choose from. The Jailhouse Inn, which used to be an old police station, is a great place to stay while you're there. If you'd like something a little elegnt, the Hotel

TOURIST

Viking is a lovely choice. If you'd like to stay close to the airport in Warwick, there is an entire street with just hotels on it. No matter where you stay, you'll be taken care of in the best ways.

29. NARRAGANSETT IS FOR TOURISTS WHO LOVE THE BEACH

If you'd like to stay near the water, but you don't feel like being in Newport, try Narragansett. There are also plenty of hotels to stay in there. The Ocean Rose Inn, Atlantic House, and Aqua Blue Hotel are as close to the water as you can get. The views of the ocean from Narragansett are absolutely beautiful and worth it.

Most parts of Narragansett are reserved for student housing so there are often parties thrown out there. The beach can get a little crowded during certain parts of the year but we can all share it. Everyone loves the beach and Narragansett beaches absolutely deliver.

You don't have to stay in a hotel to enjoy Narragansett either. You may find something amazing on AirBnB that you would prefer. However

43

you want to experience 'Gansett, make sure you're comfortable for the best experience.

30. THESE MOVIES WERE SHOT HERE

You may have heard of some of these movies: Dumb and Dumber, Moonrise Kingdom, The Great Gatsby, True Lies. What do all of these movies have in common? They all have scenes that were shot in Rhode Island!

In the movie Dumb and Dumber, you can see the famous Big Blue Bug in the background while Harry and Lloyd are cruising on the highway. The big blue bug, whose name is Nibbles Woodaway, is a Rhode Island staple and it is quite literally a big blue bug. The bug stands on top of a pest elimination company.

The movie Moonrise Kingdom actually features a few Rhode Island landmarks. Some scenes were shot in Fort Wetherill, Bayfield Farm, and the Conanicut Lighthouse. Fort Wetherill, as I mentioned above, is an old military bunker. The Conanicut Lighthouse is an inactive lighthouse located in Jamestown that is now a private residence.

The Rosecliff mansion is a very popular place to host events and apparently shoot scenes for films.

True Lies and The Great Gatsby both feature scenes from within the ballroom of the Rosecliff mansion. The movie Amistad also shot some scenes at the Rosecliff as well as the Providence State House! Rhode Island is a popular place to shoot movies, apparently.

31. NOTABLE PEOPLE FROM RHODE ISLAND

We know HP Lovecraft was from Rhode Island but he wasn't the only notable person to come out of Rhode Island. We've had some pretty interesting people come from here. Celebrities, Politicians, scientists and more have left their mark on the world.

You may have heard of Abby Aldrich Rockefeller. She was a socialite and philanthropist born in Providence RI. She may have married into the Rockefeller family but she was also known for founding the Museum of Modern Art in New York.

David Cicilline, who serves as the US Representative for Rhode Island's first congressional district, was Providence's first openly gay mayor! He was born and raised in Providence before moving to

Narragansett. He also happened to be the classmate of John F. Kennedy Jr in college.

32. VIOLA DAVIS

Viola Davis is an amazing actress who spent her life in Rhode Island. Although she was born in the South, her family lived here in Rhode Island. She grew up in Central Falls, Rhode Island with her parents and siblings.

Viola and her family lived in poverty when she was growing up. She also was very involved in performing arts while she was a student, which would explain her amazing acting abilities. Her acting resume is probably miles long.

She is an alum of Rhode Island College in Providence. Viola's life is full, and incredibly interesting. She is one of my favorite actresses and I'm so proud that she is also from this small state. Fun fact: I had class with one of her sisters! That's how small Rhode Island is!

33. FOR THE SPORTS FAN

Rhode Island also has an extensive list of Athletes that have come out of Rhode Island. There's so much talent in this small state it's almost unbelievable. Whether you're a golf fan, hockey fan, baseball fan, etc, you'll probably recognize some of these names.

Rhode Island also has local teams that need to be checked out as well. University of Rhode Island's Mens basketball games are super intense and a great way to see some Rhode Island pride come out. Except when one Rhode Island team is playing against another Rhode Island team, then watch out! There's almost nothing more intense. Check it out one time while you're in town.

Back to Athlete from Rhode Island.. some of these names may sound familiar to you. Marissa Castelli, a figure skater who is the 2017 national silver medalist. Before winning the silver, she's also won a few Bronzes. Sara DeCosta-Hayes, who won a gold medal at the 1998 winter olympics. She also won a silver medal at the 2002 winter olympics.

34. HISTORICAL LANDMARKS TO VISIT

      Rhode Island is a state with so much history that we like to show off loudly and proudly. Riding around Rhode Island, you can pass so many landmarks and probably not even know it. Here are a few that need to be visited while you're here. You won't regret soaking up all of the history this state has to offer.

      The Nelson W. Aldrich House in Providence in one historical landmark to check out. If the name Aldrich sounds familiar, it was Nelson Aldrich's daughter Abby who married into the Rockefeller family. The Aldrich house is now used as headquarters for the Rhode Island Historical Society.

      The Fleur-de-lys studios in Providence is a landmark you can't miss. The colorfulness of it makes it difficult to skip over. It's a historical art studio located in the College Hill area of Providence. It is now called the Providence Art Club and is a space still used for artists studios.

35. VISIT SOME COLLEGES WHILE YOU'RE HERE

You don't have to be a student to visit the colleges Rhode Island has to offer. Some of these colleges have beautiful campuses that practically beg to be explored. Plus, some colleges occasionally host events and forums for the public to attend. Consider visiting some of these campuses while you're exploring the state.

Salve Regina University in Newport is probably the best campus in the state to visit. The campus borders the Cliffwalk and is very close to some of the Newport Mansions. It seems silly to visit a college campus but why not when it's so close to some beautiful landscapes?

The University of Rhode Island also has a beautiful campus that's perfect for exploring. If you don't mind hills, take a tour of URI and see the beauty for yourself. The campus has some of the most beautiful contemporary architecture that just make you think of the history behind them. There are so many things to explore while you're on the URI campus.

36. RHODE ISLAND SCHOOL OF DESIGN

While we're on the topic of RI Colleges, don't think to overlook The Rhode Island School of Design. RISD is located on the East Side of Providence in the College Hill area. It is very close to Brown University and the two schools let their students sometimes intertwine their classes. It is consistently ranked as one of the best art schools in the world.

The campus of RISD spans across the East Side of Providence so it's quite hard to miss. It is an art school so expect some amazing architectural buildings and art everywhere. Walking through the campus during the fall when the leaves are falling and turning colors is an activity I strongly recommend.

RISD is a school with a lot of character. What else would you expect from an art school? They occasionally host art shows and fashion shows for the students which you don't want to miss if you're in town for one! Some extremely talented minds come out of this school and their work should be appreciated.

37. RISD MUSEUM

Yes, RISD is an art school full of amazing artists but the RISd museum features not only art from its students but art and artifacts from around the world. The museum has some of the most amazing exhibits in the world. My favorite is the Egyptian exhibit complete with mummy and sarcophagus.

The Museum features paintings, sculpture, artifacts from all time periods all over the world, and much more. Another favorite exhibit of mine is the vintage furniture exhibits set up to look like rooms inside any family home. It's truly beautiful art that you have to see to believe.

The museum also features textile such as clothing, shoes and jewelry. There's Native American clothing, Italian Clothing, Asian clothing, etc. It's one of the most amazing collections of art. A museum visit is perfect for the History fans and anyone who wants to see a giant Buddha statue! I strongly recommend a day trip to the RISD museum when you visit Rhode Island.

38. NOTABLE ALUMNI OF RISD

We know some of the most creative minds have come out of RISD. A lot of them are people we know and enjoy. Someone who immediately comes to mind is probably Seth MacFarlane. He is the creator of the show Family Guy. Yes, it's based in Rhode Island but Quahog is not a real town. You can get some tasty quahogs while you're in Rhode Island though.

James Franco is also an alum of RISD. He's best known for his roles in Spiderman, Pineapple Express, and Eat Pray Love. His resume is extensive and he's been in many films.

RISD has also gave way to people not in the film and acting business. Michael Dante DiMartino from RISD is best known for his work on Avatar; The Last Airbender. Brian Chesky, CEO of AirBnb is also an alum of RISD! Where would we be without AirBnb?

39. RHODE ISLAND THEATER COMPANIES

Rhode Island is bursting with talent and a lot of it can be found in its theaters. With so many theaters throughout the state, there's plenty of opportunities to come and witness the talent yourself. There's always something good being performed, so grab your tickets and support local theater while you're in town!

Trinity Rep and Providence Performing Arts Center are our main theater companies where the best shows have been performed. PPAC is more for traveling theater but it's still worth coming to see a show while you're in town. Trinity Rep, an award winning local theater, always has amazing shows being performed.

Rhode Island's smaller theater companies deserve recognition too! Counter Productions theater company, Burbage Theater Company, The Wilbury Theater Company, and more have so much talent and they put their all into their performances. Shows are usually on the weekend so it's the perfect time to take your loved ones to support some local RI theater. Don't forget college and high school theater productions while you're here as well!

40. AS220

On the topic of theater and art, don't forget to stop by AS220 while you're visiting. AS220 is a non profit arts organization located in downtown Providence. You may have noticed a lot of art is in Providence.. Yes, Providence is the Renaissance city and it's bursting with art. AS220 is one of those places that supports the local art through its organization.

AS220 is a space for people to come together through art and learning. Art brings people together and creates a place of wonder. Check out some of what AS220 has to offer while you're in town.

AS220 features a black box theater, a performance stage, galleries, a print shop and more. Art is what they do and it would be great for it to be supported by the community. Don't forget to support local businesses while you're here and AS220 is one that you really want to support.

41. NEW URBAN ARTS

New Urban Arts is also an organization you want to support while you're here. It is also located in Providence, not too far from AS220. It is a community studio for high school students and emerging artists. It's a safe space for people to express themselves freely through their art.

They offer volunteer opportunities for those of you who are staying a while but it's also open for people to just stop in and say hi! If you got the artist gene, consider stopping in to mentor the youth in art. If you can't volunteer, you can always show your support by donating to the cause.

NUA also has publications like newsletters, zines and art inquiry guides if you'd like to stay updated on what they're doing. They are so important to the community and deserve all of our attention and support. It is a great organization with great people so don't forget to stop and say hi on your exploration of the state.

42. WE'VE GOT FARMERS MARKETS TOO

     Aside from art, one thing Rhode Island also has a lot of is Farmers Markets. If you like fresh fruits, vegetables, and supporting local farmers, check out the farmers markets in the states. Usually open during the days on summer days, the farmers markets supply plenty of delicious foods. They are farmer run and all locally grown produce.

The Hope Street Farmers market is open May through October and accept plenty payment options. They also offer knife sharpening and live music for your convenience and entertainment. They don't just offer fruits and vegetables either! You can purchase fresh flowers, hanging flower baskets and locally grown herbs! Farmers Markets are a great addition to the communities and it is very appreciated when they are supported.

Hope Street Farmers Market also offers various aged and Rhode Island cheeses and seafood! Yes, they offer scallops, oysters, fresh fish, and lobsters. Where else would you go for the freshest seafood you can find? Look no further than a Farmers Market! Everything is fresh and local for your pleasure.

43. LOCAL BOOKSTORES NEED LOVE TOO

What other better place to support than local bookstores? Bookstores are literally treasure troves where you can find the most amazing books that you'd least expect to find. Some bookstores have amazing vintage finds like books, postcards, and even magazines.

Cellar Stories Bookstore in Providence is almost easy to miss but once you find it, you'll never want to leave. There are so many amazing things in there to find and purchase. There are books local to Rhode Island about our history that you don't want to miss out on. There are vintage novels from Shakespeare and other notable authors. They also sell vintage records and postcards. Interestingly enough, they also have vintage food menus!

Symposium books also offers some really amazing finds. They also sell vintage records and often have amazing book sales. You can also take your books there and sell them for others to enjoy. I think it would be just amazing to bring books but also buy some books. There's a chance you may not find that book again and it would be a shame to let it get away.

44. HOPE ARTISTE VILLAGE

After you put away all of your book purchases, take a visit to the Hope Artiste Village in Pawtucket. It's a small, unique business community full of interesting wonders. The Hope Artiste offers apartments, restaurants, farmers markets, and so much more!

They have great events going on all the time that are open to the public as well. The events happen occasionally so hopefully you're in town while they're getting down. Even if there aren't any events going, there are still many places within the villate to visit.

The Village offers a bakery, a bowling alley, coffee shops and more. The best thing is it's not all for those who live there. You are welcome to go bowling and enjoy some pastries and coffee. They even offer art and dance studios if you need like having a relaxing dance or paint session. There's even an escape room if you want to test your brain and skills.

45. RHODE ISLAND RUNS ON DUNKIN

Speaking of pastries, do you know how many Dunkin Donuts there are in Rhode Island? There are 124 in this whole state. We sure love our donuts and Iced Cawfees! America Runs on Dunkin? More like Rhode Island runs on Dunkin.

As someone who doesn't drink coffee, I still enjoy going to Dunkin for other items like donuts, breakfast sandwiches and coolattas. Luckily for me, I'm hardly ever too far from one. There are three in the Downtown Providence area alone. Four if you count the one in the Providence Place Mall.

However, no matter how many Dunkins we have, the Drive Thru lines are still always so packed. No matter where in the state you are, expect some lines at the Dunkins. There are even Dunkins inside other stores like Targets, Stop and Shops and etc. What is it about Dunkin that we Rhode Islanders love so much?

46. PVDONUTS

There may be 124 Dunkins in this state but there's no need to visit them when we've got our own local donut shops. PVDonuts is a relatively new donut shop that offers handmade donuts to the public. PVDonuts is an abbreviation of Providence Donuts. They are a small shop that often gets swamped with visitors every day.

The donuts are made from scratch everyday by the staff using local ingredients! The donuts are brioche donuts that can be vegan, old fashioned, cake, and cruller style donuts. I'm getting hungry just writing this. If you don't mind the line, get down here and try a one of a kind, handmade PVDonut!

At PVDonuts, they use a cake batter like mix to make the donuts lighter and airier. They also make fritters and flourless donuts there. Since the donuts are all handmade in store, the flavors occasionally switch up so I recommend you try them out more than once. They also offer more than donuts like coffee and tea. What kind of donut shop would they be if they didn't?

47. ALLIE'S DONUTS

If you don't feel like waiting in the line for a PVDonut, there's always Allie's Donuts in North Kingstown. Allie's Donuts has been around longer than PVDonuts and are an old favorite for locals. Since 1968, they've been feeding the state delicious donuts.

Their donuts are also handmade and they are famous for their extra large Big Donuts. They get swamped as well so it's best to get there early. Each day is different for them as well so you won't find anything typical about it. Allie's Donuts is definitely a stop you have to make while you're cruising through the state.

Allie's also serves breakfast and coffee, because why wouldn't they? Their most popular hours are between 9am and noon so a great time to go would be outside of that time frame. However, I think any time a day is great to enjoy a donut.

48. WE ALL SCREAM FOR ICE CREAM

Rhode Island has some of the best local ice cream and lemonade shops around. Some are even open during the winter so you don't have to miss out on the deliciousness. The cold never bothered us anyway?

One of my favorite ice cream shops is Brickleys Ice Cream in Wakefield. Their ice cream is amazing and yes, it's worth taking an hour bus ride from Providence just to go get a waffle cone with coffee oreo Ice cream. They've got so many delicious and unique flavors but the coffee oreo is my favorite. They've also got a shop in Narragansett if you're craving ice cream after being at the beach.

If you're a vegan but you still want to enjoy ice cream, Like No Udder has got you covered. During the summer, you may see their food truck on the streets or at a festival. Do yourself a favor and stop by. Don't worry, they've also got a walk in shop. Currently, they offer 12 flavors of vegan ice cream but they are always expanding and they also offer super delicious frozen lemonades.

Speaking of frozen lemonades, if you're in Rhode Island long enough, someone might try to get you involved in the old Del's vs Mr Lemon debate. Dels and Mr Lemon are two local and very popular frozen lemonade states that we Rhode Islanders can't decide which is better. I myself am biased towards Mr Lemon but both shops are pretty great and refreshing in the sweltering summers. Give them a try yourself when you get a chance.

49. FOOD TRUCK FESTIVALS

Here in Rhode Island, you may often see a food truck hanging out somewhere. I strongly recommend you try one out. If you're here long enough, try them all! Sometimes you may see a few camped out in the Providence downtown area. They offer burgers, hot dogs, and even Korean food! Every other Friday, Roger Williams Park hosts a food truck festival where you can go through the stress of trying to choose one food truck to eat from.

My personal favorite is the Poco Loco taco truck. Their tacos and burritos are amazing, and I strongly recommend them. Although I'd stay away from the hot sauce if you can't stand the heat. It's delicious but it's not for the weak tongued individual. The burritos and tacos are super filling and you won't find yourself looking around for more food that long after eating one.

If you're into interesting foods, there's a food truck called Open Season you might like. Does Bison burgers and venison chili cheese fries sound like something you might like? Say you're in the mood for BBQ. There's a truck for that too! Baby's Bonetown BBQ will take good care of your stomach.

50. HAVEN BROS

Last but not least, our most famous food truck: The Haven Brothers Diner. You've probably never seen a food truck with a small sit in diner and an order window! And yes, it is a food truck! They park downtown next to City Hall every night and serve the population. The best part is they stay open late. They're a favorite for the late night after the club crowd.

Haven Bros has been around since 1893 when they were a horse drawn carriage! They are one of the oldest restaurants on wheels and we just love them here. The staff are so amazing and sweet. How cool is this: Haven Bros was featured on Family Guy as a cartoon! The history alone should be enough to get you to come and try it out.

Okay, let's talk about the food. It's amazing! I love myself a good Murder Burger and I can gobble it up within minutes. They also offer hot dogs, mozzarella sticks, tenders, grilled cheese, onion rings and so much more. They even offer a garbage plate which is anything BUT garbage! It is a plate with chicken tenders, mozzarella sticks and fries smothered in nacho cheese. If that's not enough to get you to come and try Haven Bros I don't know what is.

TOP REASONS TO BOOK THIS TRIP

Diversity: There's a place for everyone and everyone has a place. We welcome you with open arms.

History: The state is full of historical tidbits that you only have to see to believe.

Food: We've got amazing food here! I've explained so much but you have to come try it for yourself.

BONUS BOOK

50 THINGS TO KNOW ABOUT PACKING LIGHT FOR TRAVEL

PACK THE RIGHT WAY EVERY TIME

AUTHOR: MANIDIPA BHATTACHARYYA

Edited by Melanie Howthorne

ABOUT THE AUTHOR

Manidipa Bhattacharyya is a creative writer and editor, with an
education in English literature and Linguistics. After working in the IT
industry for seven long years she decided to call it quits and follow her
heart instead. Manidipa has been ghost writing, editing, proof reading
and doing secondary research services for many story tellers and article
writers for about three years. She stays in Kolkata, India with her
husband and a busy two year old. In her own time Manidipa enjoys
travelling, photography and writing flash fiction.

Manidipa believes in travelling light and never carries anything that she
couldn't haul herself on a trip. However, travelling with her child
changed the scenario. She seemed to carry the entire world with her for
the baby on the first two trips. But good sense prevailed and she is
again working her way to becoming a light traveler, this time with a
kid.

INTRODUCTION

He who would travel happily
must travel light.

-Antoine de Saint-Exupéry

Travel takes you to different places from seas and mountains to deserts and much more. In your travels you get to interact with different people and their cultures. You will, however, enjoy the sights and interact positively with these new people even more, if you are travelling light.

When you travel light your mind can be free from worry about your belongings. You do not have to spend precious vacation time waiting for your luggage to arrive after a long flight. There is be no chance of your bags going missing and the best part is that you need not pay a fee for checked baggage.

People who have mastered this art of packing light will root for you to take only one carry-on, wherever you go. However, many people can find it really hard to pack light. More so if you are travelling with children. Differentiating between "must have" and "just in case" items is the starting point. There will be ample shopping avenues at your destination which are just waiting to be explored.

This book will show you 'packing' in a new 'light' – pun intended – and help you to embrace light packing practices for all of your future travels.

Off to packing!

DEDICATION

I dedicate this book to all the travel buffs that I know, who have given me great insights into the contents of their backpacks.

THE RIGHT TRAVEL GEAR

1. CHOOSE YOUR TRAVEL GEAR CAREFULLY

While selecting your travel gear, pick items that are light weight, durable and most importantly, easy to carry. There are cases with wheels so you can drag them along – these are usually on the heavy side because of the trolley. Alternatively a backpack that you can carry comfortably on your back, or even a duffel bag that you can carry easily by hand or sling across your body are also great options. Whatever you choose, one thing to keep in mind is that the luggage itself should not weigh a ton, this will give you the flexibility to bring along one extra pair of shoes if you so desire.

2. CARRY THE MINIMUM NUMBER OF BAGS

Selecting light weight luggage is not everything. You need to restrict the number of bags you carry as well. One carry-on size bag is ideal for light travel. Most carriers allow one cabin baggage plus one purse, handbag or camera bag as long as it slides under the seat in front. So technically, you can carry two items of luggage without checking them in.

3. PACK ONE EXTRA BAG

Always pack one extra empty bag along with your essential items. This could be a very light weight duffel bag or even a sturdy tote bag which takes up minimal space. In the event that you end up buying a lot of souvenirs, you already have a handy bag to stuff all that into and do not have to spend time hunting for an appropriate bag.

I'm very strict with my packing and have everything in its right place. I never change a rule. I hardly use anything in the hotel room. I wheel my own wardrobe in and that's it.

CLOTHES & ACCESSORIES

4. PLAN AHEAD

Figure out in advance what you plan to do on your trip. That will help you to pick that one dress you need for the occasion. If you are going to attend a wedding then you have to carry formal wear. If not, you can ditch the gown for something lighter that will be comfortable during long walks or on the beach.

5. WEAR THAT JACKET

Remember that wearing items will not add extra luggage for your air travel. So wear that bulky jacket that you plan to carry for your trip. This saves space and can also help keep you warm during the chilly flight.

6. MIX AND MATCH

Carry clothes that can be interchangeably used to reinvent your look. Find one top that goes well with a couple of pairs of pants or skirts. Use tops, shirts and jackets wisely along with other accessories like a scarf or a stole to create a new look.

7. CHOOSE YOUR FABRIC WISELY

Stuffing clothes in cramped bags definitely takes its toll which results in wrinkles. It is best to carry wrinkle free, synthetic clothes or merino tops. This will eliminate the need for that small iron you usually bring along.

8. DITCH CLOTHES PACK UNDERWEAR

Pack more underwear and socks. These are the things that will give you a fresh feel even if you do not get a chance to wear fresh clothes. Moreover these are easy to wash and can be dried inside the hotel room itself.

9. CHOOSE DARK OVER LIGHT

While picking your clothes choose dark coloured ones. They are easy to colour coordinate and can last longer before needing a wash. Accidental food spills and dirt from the road are less visible on darker clothes.

10. WEAR YOUR JEANS

Take only one pair of Jeans with you, which you should wear on the flight. Remember to pick a pair that can be worn for sightseeing trips and is equally eloquent for dinner. You can add variety by adding light weight cargoes and chinos.

11. CARRY SMART ACCESSORIES

The right accessory can give you a fresh look even with the same old dress. An intelligent neck-piece, a couple of bright scarves, stoles or a sarong can be used in a number of ways to add variety to your clothing. These light weight beauties can double up as a nursing cover, a light blanket, beach wear, a modesty cover for visiting places of worship, and also makes for an enthralling game of peek-a-boo.

12. LEARN TO FOLD YOUR GARMENTS

Seasoned travellers all swear by rolling their clothes for compact and wrinkle free packing. Bundle packing, where you roll the clothes around a central object as if tying it up, is also a popular method of compact and wrinkle free packing. Stacking folded clothes one on top of another is a big no-no as it makes creases extreme and they are difficult to get rid of without ironing.

13. WASH YOUR DIRTY LAUNDRY

One of the ways to avoid carrying loads of clothes is to wash the clothes you carry. At some places you might get to use the laundry services or a Laundromat but if you are in a pinch, best solution is to wash them yourself. If that is the plan then carrying quick drying clothes is highly recommended, which most often also happen to be the wrinkle free variety.

14. LEAVE THOSE TOWELS BEHIND

Regular towels take up a lot of space, are heavy and take ages to dry out. If you are staying at hotels they will provide you with towels anyway. If you are travelling to a remote place, where the availability of towels look doubtful, carry a light weight travel towel of viscose material to do the job.

15. USE A COMPRESSION BAG

Compression bags are getting lots of recommendation now days from regular travellers. These are useful for saving space in your luggage when you have to pack bulky dresses. While packing for the return trip, get help from the hotel staff to arrange a vacuum cleaner.

FOOTWEAR

16. PUT ON YOUR HIKING BOOTS

If you have plans to go hiking or trekking during your trip, you will need those bulky hiking boots. The best way to carry them is to wear them on flight to save space and luggage weight. You can remove the boots once inside and be comfortable in your socks.

17. PICKING THE RIGHT SHOES

Shoes are often the bulkiest items, along with being the dainty if you are a female. They need care and take up a lot of space in your luggage. It is advisable therefore to pick shoes very carefully. If you plan to do a lot of walking and site seeing, then wearing a pair of comfortable walking shoes are a must. For more formal occasions you can carry durable, light weight flats which will not take up much space.

18. STUFF SHOES

If you happen to pack a pair of shoes, ensure you utilize their hollow insides. Tuck small items like rolled up socks or belts to save space. They will also be easy to find.

TOILETRIES

19. STASHING TOILETRIES

Carry only absolute necessities. Airline rules dictate
that for one carry-on bag, liquids and gels must be in
3.4 ounce (100ml) bottles or less, and must be packed
in a one quart zip-lock bag. If you are planning to stay
in a hotel, the basic things will be provided for you.
It's best is to buy the rest from the local market at
your destination.

20. TAKE ALONG TAMPONS

Tampons are a hard to find item in a lot of countries.
Figure out how many you need and pack accordingly.
For longer stays you can buy them online and have
them delivered to where you are staying.

21. GET PAMPERED BEFORE YOU TRAVEL

Some avid travellers suggest getting a pedicure and
manicure just the day before travelling. This not only
gives you a well kept look, you also save the trouble
of packing nail polish. Remember, every little bit of
weight reduced adds up.

ELECTRONICS
22. LUGGING ALONG ELECTRONICS

Electronics have a large role to play in our lives today. Most of us cannot imagine our lives away from our phones, laptops or tablets. However while travelling, one must consider the amount of weight these electronics add to our luggage. Thankfully smart phones come along with all the essentials tools like a camera, email access, picture editing tools and more. They are smart to the point of eliminating the need to carry multiple gadgets. Choose a smart phone that suits all your requirements and travel with the world in your palms or pocket.

23. REDUCE THE NUMBER OF CHARGERS

If you do travel with multiple electronic devices, you will have to bear the additional burden of carrying all their chargers too. Check if a single charger can be used for multiple devices. You might also consider investing in a pocket charger. These small devices support multiple devices while keeping you charged on the go.

24. TRAVEL FRIENDLY APPS

Along with smart phones come numerous apps, which are immensely helpful in our travels. You name it and you have an app for it at hand – take pictures, sharing with friends and family, torch to light dark roads, maps, checking flight/train times, find hotels and many other things. Use these smart alternatives to traditional items like books to eliminate weight and save space.

I get ideas about what's essential when packing my suitcase.

-Diane von Furstenberg

TRAVELLING WITH KIDS

25. BRING ALONG THE STROLLER

Kids might enjoy walking for a while but they soon tire out and a stroller is the just the right thing for them to rest in while you continue your tour. Strollers also double duty as a luggage carrier and shopping bag holder. Remember to pick a light weight, easy to handle brand of stroller. Better yet, find out in advance if you can rent a stroller at your destination.

26. BRING ONLY ENOUGH DIAPERS FOR YOUR TRIP

Diapers take up a lot of space and add to the weight of your luggage. Therefore it is advisable to carry just enough diapers to last through the trip and a few for afterwards, till you buy fresh stock at your destination. Unless of course you are travelling to a really remote area, in which case you have no choice but to carry the load. Otherwise diapers are something you will find pretty easily.

27. TAKE ONLY A COUPLE OF TOYS

Children are easily attracted by new things in their environment. While travelling they will find numerous 'new' objects to scrutinize and play with. Packing just one favorite toy is enough, or if there is no favorite toy leave out all of them in favor of stories or imaginary games.

28. CARRY KID FRIENDLY SNACKS

Create a small snack counter in your bag to store away quick bites for those sudden hunger pangs. Depending on the child's age this could include chocolates, raisins, dry fruits, granola bars or biscuits. Also keep a bottle of water handy for your little one.

These things do not add much weight and can be adjusted in a handbag or knapsack.

29. GAMES TO CARRY

Create some travel specific, imaginary games if you have slightly grown up children, like spot the attractions. Keep a coloring book and colors handy for in-flight or hotel time. Apps on your smart phone can keep the children engaged with cartoons and story books. Older children are often entertained by games available on phones or tablets. This cuts the weight of luggage down while keeping the kids entertained.

30. LET THE KIDS CARRY THEIR LOAD

A good thing is to start early sharing of responsibilities. Let your child pick a bag of his or her choice and pack it themselves. Keep tabs on what they are stuffing in their bags by asking if they will be using that item on the trip. It could start out being just an entertainment bag initially but with growing years they will learn to sort the useful from the superfluous. Children as little as four can maneuver a small trolley suitcase like a pro- their experience in pull along toys credit. If you are worried that you may be pulling it for them, you may want to start with a backpack.

31. DECIDE ON LOCATION FOR CHILDREN TO SLEEP

While on a trip you might not always get a crib at your destination, and carrying one will make life all the more difficult. Instead call ahead to see if there are any cribs or roll out beds for children. You may even put blankets on the floor. Weave them a story about camping and they will gladly sleep without any trouble.

32. GET BABY PRODUCTS DELIVERED AT YOUR DESTINATION

If you are absolutely paranoid about not getting your favourite variety of diaper or brand of baby food, check out online stores like amazon.com for services in your destination city. You can buy things online ahead of your travel and get them delivered to your hotel upon arrival.

33. FEEDING NEEDS OF YOUR INFANTS

If you are travelling with a breastfed infant, you save the trouble of carrying bottles and bottle sanitization kits. For special food, or medications, you may need to call ahead to make sure you have a refrigerator where you are staying.

34. FEEDING NEEDS OF YOUR TODDLER

With the progression from infancy to toddler, their dietary requirements too evolve. You will have to pack some snacks for travelling time. Fresh fruits and vegetables can be purchased at your destination. Most of the cities you travel to in whichever part of the world, will have baby food products and formulas, available at the local drug-store or the supermarket.

35. PICKING CLOTHES FOR YOUR BABY

Contrary to popular belief, babies can do without many changes of clothes. At the most pack 2 outfits per day. Pack mix and match type clothes for your little one as well. Pick things which are comfortable to wear and quick to dry.

36. SELECTING SHOES FOR YOUR BABY

Like outfits, kids can make do with two pairs of comfortable shoes. If you can get some water resistant shoes it will be best. To expedite drying wet shoes, you can stuff newspaper in them then wrap them with newspaper and leave them to dry overnight.

37. KEEP ONE CHANGE OF CLOTHES HANDY

Travelling with kids can be tricky. Keep a change of clothes for the kids and mum handy in your purse or tote bag. This takes a bit of space in your hand luggage but comes extremely handy in case there are any accidents or spills.

38. LEAVE BEHIND BABY ACCESSORIES

Baby accessories like their bed, bath tub, car seat, crib etc. should be left at home. Many hotels provide a crib on request, while car seats can be borrowed from friends or rented. Babies can be given a bath in the hotel sink or even in the adult bath tub with a little bit of water. If you bring a few bath toys, they can be used in the bath, pool, and out of water. They can also be sanitized easily in the sink.

39. CARRY A SMALL LOAD OF PLASTIC BAGS

With children around there are chances of a number of soiled clothes and diapers. These plastic bags help to sort the dirt from the clean inside your big bag. These are very light weight and come in handy to other carry stuff as well at times.

PACK WITH A PURPOSE

40. PACKING FOR BUSINESS TRIPS

One neutral-colored suit should suffice. It can be paired with different shirts, ties and accessories for different occasions. One pair of black suit pants could be worn with a matching jacket for the office or with a snazzy top for dinner.

41. PACKING FOR A CRUISE

Most cruises have formal dinners, and that formal dress usually takes up a lot of space. However you might find a tuxedo to rent. For women, a short black dress with multiple accessory options will do the trick.

42. PACKING FOR A LONG TRIP OVER DIFFERENT CLIMATES

The secret packing mantra for travel over multiple climates is layering. Layering traps air around your body creating insulation against the cold. The same light t-shirt that is comfortable in a warmer climate can be the innermost layer in a colder climate.

REDUCE SOME MORE WEIGHT

43. LEAVE PRECIOUS THINGS AT HOME

Things that you would hate to lose or get damaged leave them at home. Precious jewelry, expensive gadgets or dresses, could be anything. You will not require these on your trip. Leave them at home and spare the load on your mind.

44. SEND SOUVENIRS BY MAIL

If you have spent all your money on purchasing souvenirs, carrying them back in the same bag that you brought along would be difficult. Either pack everything in another bag and check it in the airport or get everything shipped to your home. Use an international carrier for a secure transit, but this could be more expensive than the checking fees at the airport.

45. AVOID CARRYING BOOKS

Books equal to weight. There are many reading apps which you can download on your smart phone or tab. Plus there are gadgets like Kindle and Nook that are thinner and lighter alternatives to your regular book.

CHECK, GET, SET, CHECK AGAIN

46. STRATEGIZE BEFORE PACKING

Create a travel list and prepare all that you think you need to carry along. Keep everything on your bed or floor before packing and then think through once again – do I really need that? Any item that meets this question can be avoided. Remove whatever you don't really need and pack the rest.

47. TEST YOUR LUGGAGE

Once you have fully packed for the trip take a test trip with your luggage. Take your bags and go to town for window shopping for an hour. If you enjoy your hour long trip it is good to go, if not, go home and reduce the load some more. Repeat this test till you hit the right weight.

48. ADD A ROLL OF DUCT TAPE

You might wonder why, when this book has been talking about reducing stuff, we're suddenly asking you to pack something totally unusual. This is because when you have limited supplies, duct tape is immensely helpful for small repairs – a broken bag, leaking zip-lock bag, broken sunglasses, you name it and duct tape can fix it, temporarily.

49. LIST OF ESSENTIAL ITEMS

Even though the emphasis is on packing light, there are things which have to be carried for any trip. Here is our list of essentials:

- Passport/Visa or any other ID

- Any other paper work that might be required on a trip like permits, hotel reservation confirmations etc.

- Medicines – all your prescription medicines and emergency kit, especially if you are travelling with children

- Medical or vaccination records

- Money in foreign currency if travelling to a different country

- Tickets- Email or Message them to your phone

50. MAKE THE MOST OF YOUR TRIP

Wherever you are going, whatever you hope to do we encourage you to embrace it whole-heartedly. Take in the scenery, the culture and above all, enjoy your time away from home.

>TOURIST

*On a long journey even a straw
weighs heavy.*

-Spanish Proverb

PACKING AND PLANNING TIPS

A Week before Leaving

- Arrange for someone to take care of pets and water plants

- Stop mail and newspaper

- Notify Credit Card companies where you are going.

- Change your thermostat settings

- Car inspected, oil is changed, and tires have the correct pressure.

- Passports and id is up to date.

- Pay bills.

- Copy important items and download travel Apps.

- Start collecting small bills for tips

Right Before Leaving

- Clean out refrigerator.

- Empty garbage cans.

- Lock windows.

- Make sure you have the right ID with you.

- Bring cash for tips.

- Remember travel documents.

- Lock door behind you.

- Remember wallet.

- Unplug items in house and pack chargers.

READ OTHER
GREATER THAN A TOURIST
BOOKS

Greater Than a Tourist San Miguel de Allende Guanajuato Mexico:
50 Travel Tips from a Local by Tom Peterson

Greater Than a Tourist – Lake George Area New York USA:
50 Travel Tips from a Local by Janine Hirschklau

Greater Than a Tourist – Monterey California United States:
50 Travel Tips from a Local by Katie Begley

Greater Than a Tourist – Chanai Crete Greece:
50 Travel Tips from a Local by Dimitra Papagrigoraki

Greater Than a Tourist – The Garden Route Western Cape Province
South Africa:
50 Travel Tips from a Local by Li-Anne McGregor van Aardt

Greater Than a Tourist – Sevilla Andalusia Spain:
50 Travel Tips from a Local by Gabi Gazon

Greater Than a Tourist – Kota Bharu Kelantan Malaysia:
50 Travel Tips from a Local by Aditi Shukla

Children's Book: Charlie the Cavalier Travels the World by Lisa
Rusczyk

> TOURIST

Visit Greater Than a Tourist for Free Travel Tips
http://GreaterThanATourist.com

Sign up for the Greater Than a Tourist Newsletter for
discount days, new books, and travel information:
http://eepurl.com/cxspyf

Follow us on Facebook for tips, images, and ideas:
https://www.facebook.com/GreaterThanATourist

Follow us on Pinterest for travel tips and ideas:
http://pinterest.com/GreaterThanATourist

Follow us on Instagram for beautiful travel images:
http://Instagram.com/GreaterThanATourist

> TOURIST

Please leave your honest review of this book on Amazon and Goodreads. Please send your feedback to GreaterThanaTourist@gmail.com as we continue to improve the series. Thank you. We appreciate your positive and constructive feedback. Thank you.

METRIC CONVERSIONS

TEMPERATURE

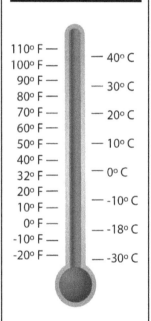

110° F —
100° F —
90° F —
80° F —
70° F —
60° F —
50° F —
40° F —
32° F —
20° F —
10° F —
0° F —
-10° F —
-20° F —

— 40° C
— 30° C
— 20° C
— 10° C
— 0° C
— -10° C
— -18° C
— -30° C

To convert F to C:

Subtract 32, and then multiply by 5/9 or .5555.

To Convert C to F:

Multiply by 1.8 and then add 32.

32F = 0C

LIQUID VOLUME

To Convert:..................Multiply by
U.S. Gallons to Liters................ 3.8
U.S. Liters to Gallons 26
Imperial Gallons to U.S. Gallons 1.2
Imperial Gallons to Liters....... 4.55
Liters to Imperial Gallons 22
1 Liter = .26 U.S. Gallon
1 U.S. Gallon = 3.8 Liters

DISTANCE

To convert ....Multiply by
Inches to Centimeters 2.54
Centimeters to Inches 39
Feet to Meters...................... .3
Meters to Feet 3.28
Yards to Meters 91
Meters to Yards 1.09
Miles to Kilometers 1.61
Kilometers to Miles............ .62
1 Mile = 1.6 km
1 km = .62 Miles

WEIGHT

1 Ounce = .28 Grams
1 Pound = .4555 Kilograms
1 Gram = .04 Ounce
1 Kilogram = 2.2 Pounds

TRAVEL QUESTIONS

- Do you bring presents home to family or friends after a vacation?

- Do you get motion sick?

- Do you have a favorite billboard?

- Do you know what to do if there is a flat tire?

- Do you like a sun roof open?

- Do you like to eat in the car?

- Do you like to wear sun glasses in the car?

- Do you like toppings on your ice cream?

- Do you use public bathrooms?

- Did you bring your cell phone and does it have power?

- Do you have a form of identification with you?

- Have you ever been pulled over by a cop?

- Have you ever given money to a stranger on a road trip?

- Have you ever taken a road trip with animals?

- Have you ever went on a vacation alone?

- Have you ever run out of gas?

- If you could move to any place in the world, where would it be?

- If you could travel anywhere in the world, where would you travel?

- If you could travel in any vehicle, which one would it be?

- If you had three things to wish for from a magic genie, what would they be?

- If you have a driver's license, how many times did it take you to pass the test?

- What are you the most afraid of on vacation?

- What do you want to get away from the most when you are on vacation?

- What foods smells bad to you?

- What item to you bring on ever trip with you away from home?

- What makes you sleepy?

- What song would you love to hear on the radio when you're cruising on the highway?

- What travel job would you want the least?

- What will you miss most while you are away from home?

- What is something you always wanted to try?

- What is the best road side attraction that you ever saw?

- What is the farthest distance you ever biked?

- What is the farthest distance you ever walked?

- What is the weirdest thing you needed to buy while on vacation?

- What is your favorite candy?

- What is your favorite color car?

- What is your favorite family vacation?

- What is your favorite food in the world?

- What is your favorite gas station drink or food?

- What is your favorite license plate design?

- What is your favorite restaurant in the world?

- What is your favorite smell?

- What is your favorite song?

- What is your favorite sound that nature makes?

- What is your favorite thing to bring home from a vacation?

- What is your favorite vacation with friends?

- What is your favorite way to relax?

- What is your favorite weather conditions while driving?

- Where in the world would you rather never get to travel?

- Where is the farthest place you ever traveled in a car?

- Where is the farthest place you ever went North, South, East and West?

- Where is your favorite place in the world?

- Who is your favorite singer?

- Who taught you how to drive?

- Who will you miss the most while you are away?

- Who if the first person you will call when you get to your destination?

- Who brought you on your first vacation?

- Who likes to travel the most in your life?

- Would you rather be hot or cold?

- Would you rather drive above, below, or at the speed limited?

- Would you rather drive on a highway or a back road?

- Would you rather go on a train or a boat?

- Would you rather go to the beach or the woods?

TRAVEL BUCKET LIST

NOTES